WONDER WOMAN™ MYTHOLOGY

Wonder Woman and the Heroes of Myth

by STEVE KORTÉ

Wonder Woman created by William Moulton Marston

Consultant:
Laurel Bowman
Department of Greek and Roman Studies
University of Victoria
British Columbia, Canada

CAPSTONE PRESS
a capstone imprint

Published by Capstone Press in 2017
1710 Roe Crest Drive
North Mankato, Minnesota 56003
www.mycapstone.com

STAR37674

Library of Congress Cataloging-in-Publication Data is available on
the Library of Congress website.

ISBN: 978-1-5157-4585-3 (library binding)
ISBN: 978-1-5157-4598-3 (eBook PDF)

Summary: Introduces a variety of heroes from Greek, Roman,
Egyptian, and other world mythologies, and explores how they are
woven into the fabric of Wonder Woman's backstory.

Editor: Christopher Harbo

Designer: Tracy McCabe

Creative Director: Bob Lentz

Production Specialist: Katy LaVigne

Image Credits:
Capstone: C.E. Richards, 28, James Nathan, 11, José Alfonso
Ocampo Ruiz, 24, Nadine Takvorian, 15, Scott Altman, 8, 12,
19, 21, 22; Shutterstock: Andrea Izzotti, 16, Artem Loskutnikov,
17, Artem Loskutnikov, cover (bottom right), aslysun, 28 (inset),
Christos Georghiou, cover, (left), George W. Bailey, 11 (inset),
Mikhail Bakunovich, 13, Sergej Razvodovskij, cover, (top right),
Vectomart, cover (bottom), 27, Vuk Kostic, 7; Warner Brothers,
throughout (Wonder Woman and backgrounds)

Printed and bound in the USA.
010061S17

TABLE OF CONTENTS

A Hero Among Heroes

Myths are astonishing tales of heroes and villains from around the world. Many myths are centuries old and have been passed down from generation to generation. The gods and goddesses of Greek mythology were **immortal** beings who had enormous power over every creature on Earth, including **mortal** men and women. Some of the gods and goddesses used their powers for evil and caused problems for mortals. Others were true heroes. They cared for the human race and helped people in times of need.

In the stories of Wonder Woman, the Greek gods created a race of brave women known as the Amazons. Although the Amazons were skilled warriors, they chose to live peacefully on a secret island. When a nuclear war threatened to destroy our world, the Amazons selected a champion to save us. She was Princess Diana, and she would later win fame as Wonder Woman.

The tales of Wonder Woman are filled with dangerous adventures and heroic deeds. Her stories also allow us to meet some of the greatest mythological heroes of all time. From Superman and Batman to Hercules and Zeus, the heroes of myth have all been linked to the life of Wonder Woman.

immortal—able to live forever

mortal—human, referring to a being who will eventually die

CHAPTER 1
Rulers of the Gods

ZEUS

Zeus was the incredibly powerful king of the Greek gods. He ruled Mount Olympus, the tall mountain above Greece where the gods lived. Zeus had claimed the throne atop Olympus after he and his brothers and sisters led a war against their evil father, Cronus. They defeated Cronus, and then Zeus and his brothers divided the realm between themselves. Zeus ruled the sky, Poseidon took the sea, and Hades ruled the underworld.

Zeus also ruled the weather. He would hurl thunderbolts down at the mortals below when they displeased him. In addition, Zeus was the god of hospitality and oaths. He watched over the bonds between hosts and guests, and the promises between people. He punished anyone that broke these bonds or oaths. Most importantly, he was the god who gave kings on Earth the authority to rule.

In the stories of Wonder Woman, Zeus did not take part in the creation of the Amazons. Instead, five goddesses gave life to the peace-loving tribe. Eventually, Zeus came to appreciate the Amazons and their mission to inspire Earth's mortals to pursue truth and justice. Centuries later, when Princess Diana became Wonder Woman, she received indestructible bracelets. They were **forged** from pieces of Zeus' magic shield.

forge—to form something from metal using heat or a hammer

FACT
In Roman mythology, Zeus was known as Jupiter.

HERA

Hera was the Greek goddess of women, marriage, and childbirth. Although she held a lofty position, Hera was always jealous of Zeus, Poseidon, and Hades. Despite her feelings, Hera sat beside Zeus' throne as his queen and wife. They even had several children, including the war god Ares.

However, their marriage was not a happy one. Zeus fell in love with many other women, which always drove Hera into a jealous frenzy. For most of their time together, Hera kept busy plotting **revenge** on Zeus.

In Wonder Woman's world, Hera was against the creation of the Amazons at first, perhaps because it was not her idea. Centuries later, though, she grew impressed with Diana's skills and often came to her aid. Most remarkably, she brought Diana back to life after she was murdered by the demon Neron. Hera even offered to make Diana the goddess of truth on Mount Olympus. Though flattered by the offer, Diana returned to the world of mortals to continue in her role as Wonder Woman.

FACT

When Wonder Woman was excited, she would often exclaim, "Great Hera!"

FACT

In ancient Greece, artists often showed Hera carrying a scepter. Perched on top of this staff was a cuckoo bird, which was Hera's favorite bird.

revenge—an action taken to repay harm done

CHAPTER 2

Powerful Goddesses

ATHENA

Athena was the Greek goddess of war, wisdom, and the arts. She was a powerful goddess of battle strategy who dressed in fine armor. She also enjoyed a special status as the favorite child of the great god Zeus. In fact, Zeus loved Athena as deeply as he despised his son, the war god Ares.

Athena and her brother, Ares, were bitter **rivals**. Yet, whenever they met in combat, Athena always easily defeated her brother. As the god of battle strategy, she always had the upper hand on Ares, the god of battle frenzy. One example of this was in the *Iliad* by the poet Homer. It told of a battle between Ares and the warrior Diomedes. Athena came to the aid of Diomedes and helped guide his spear into Ares' stomach. This sent the war god running away in pain.

Long before Wonder Woman was born, Ares tricked the hero Hercules. Ares convinced Hercules and his army to attack and destroy the Amazon city of Themyscira. Half of the Amazons declared war on Hercules. The other half, led by Queen Hippolyta, moved to a secret island, where they built a perfect, peaceful society. Athena rewarded the peace-loving Amazons with immortality. Centuries later, Athena granted wisdom to the newborn Princess Diana. She even crafted Wonder Woman's ceremonial golden suit of armor.

rival—someone whom a person competes against

A HOLLOW HORSE

Athena sometimes whispered battle advice to mortals. During the Trojan War, Athena suggested that the Greeks present a giant wooden horse to their foes, the Trojans. The Greeks claimed that it was a peace offering. When the Trojans brought the horse inside their city walls, Greek soldiers sprang from the horse's hollow belly to defeat their enemy.

HESTIA

Hestia was the goddess of home and family in Greek mythology. Although she did not appear in as many myths as some of the other **deities** on Mount Olympus, Hestia was widely worshipped by families in ancient Greece.

Hestia valued peace above all. Although Athena fought in some wars, Hestia refused to get involved in any type of conflict. Her strong desire for peace also led her to turn her back on marriage — a surprising choice for the goddess of family. Her decision came after two gods started fighting for her hand in marriage. One was the sea god Poseidon, and the other was Apollo, the god of music. Hestia feared their fight could lead to a full-scale war, so she asked Zeus for help. The mighty god allowed Hestia to reject marriage forever.

When Princess Diana became Wonder Woman, she received many priceless gifts. These included her bullet-deflecting bracelets and a golden suit of armor. The most important gift of all came from Hestia. It was the magical Lasso of Truth. The golden lasso was indestructible. Even better, anyone that Wonder Woman bound within the lasso was forced to tell the truth.

ROMAN FIRES

In Roman mythology, Hestia was known as Vesta. An **eternal** flame was lit in her temple in the center of Rome. It was a high honor for young girls, often only six years old, to be chosen as temple workers. For the next 30 years, they were required to keep the temple flame burning.

deity—a god or goddess
eternal—lasting forever

ARTEMIS

Artemis was the Greek goddess of hunting and nature. She was also the chief goddess worshipped by the Amazons. Like the Amazons, Artemis wanted no contact with men. In fact, she didn't even wish to be seen by men. In addition, Artemis was a highly skilled archer. She drove a chariot that was followed by a pack of immortal dogs as she hunted for deer and wild boar.

In the world of Wonder Woman, several women have been known as Artemis. The first was the Greek goddess of mythology, who joined with four other goddesses to create the new race of peace-loving women. She gave the women great hunting skills, and it was this Artemis who named them the Amazons.

Another Artemis was a member of the warrior tribe of Amazons that broke away from the peace-loving Amazons on Themyscira. This Artemis was raised in the Egyptian city of Bana-Mighdall, where she became an expert fighter. Later, after the two Amazon tribes rejoined forces, Artemis won a contest to become the new Wonder Woman. She died battling the villainous White Magician, but the original Wonder Woman rescued her from the realm of Hades.

BAST

There is a joke that says, "In Ancient Egypt, cats were worshipped as gods. Cats have never forgotten this." Cats were indeed highly honored in Egypt. They were considered important family members. In addition, one of the most beloved Egyptian goddesses was Bast, who had the body of a woman and the head of a cat. Bast was the goddess of pleasure and plenty. Egyptians worshipped her and held huge feasts in her honor.

Bast controlled all of the cats on Earth, and it was widely thought that her cat-servants brought good luck to mortals. Some even believed that if a fire broke out in a home, the family cat would jump into the flames. The cat would then absorb the fire into its body and save the household from destruction.

In Wonder Woman **lore**, Bast was worshipped by the Egyptian tribe of Amazons that lived in Bana-Mighdall. Years later, these Amazons reunited with Queen Hippolyta's followers on the island of Themyscira. Together, they joined with the super heroes of Earth to fight a galaxy-threatening alien known as Imperiex. The heroes won, but Themyscira was destroyed during the battle. Bast came to the rescue. She helped to build a magical, floating island known as New Themyscira.

FELINE FRIENDS

Egyptians loved their cats so much that they would shave off their eyebrows to **mourn** a family cat that died. Mummified cats were also buried alongside people.
In the town of Bubastis, which translates as "Bast's place," tens of thousands of cat mummies have been discovered.

lore—stories passed down over generations

mourn—to be very sad and miss someone who has died

MAMMITU

Thousands of years ago in ancient Mesopotamia, tales were told of the Babylonian goddess of fate. Her name was Mammitu, and she had the body of a woman and the head of a goat. She lived in the underworld, where she controlled the lives of all mortals, from birth to death. It was Mammitu who determined the fate of every newborn child. Whatever Mammitu decided would always come to pass. At the end of a person's life, she would then pass judgments on the dead.

In Wonder Woman's world, Mammitu was also worshipped by the Bana-Mighdall Amazons. She joined Bast and helped the Amazons build New Themyscira after their first island was destroyed during the Imperiex War.

solemn—very serious

18

New Themyscira was a wondrous collection of islands that
floated above the mysterious Bermuda Triangle in the Atlantic
Ocean. In a **solemn** ceremony, all of the goddesses promised to
defend this new home of the Amazons. Mammitu then declared
that no god or mortal would ever be able to force a goddess to
break that promise.

CHAPTER 3
Amazing Amazons

HIPPOLYTA

In Greek mythology, Hippolyta was the daughter of Ares, the god of war. She was also the queen of the Amazons. As a symbol of her rule, she wore a golden belt. This belt, given by her father, marked Hippolyta as the greatest Amazon warrior. Unfortunately, it also led to her doom.

The hero Hercules was required to perform 12 difficult tasks, known as labors. One of his tasks was to bring Hippolyta's belt to King Eurystheus. When Hercules encountered Hippolyta and her warriors, he expected a fight. To his surprise, they welcomed him instead. Even more shocking, Hippolyta liked Hercules so much she simply offered him the belt as a gift.

Meanwhile, the goddess Hera didn't want Hercules to complete his task. She disguised herself as an Amazonian warrior. Then she spread a rumor that Hercules planned to kidnap the queen. Outraged, Hippolyta's warriors attacked Hercules. Their ambush made him think that Hippolyta had betrayed him. In anger, he killed her and stole the belt before fleeing from the attacking Amazons.

FACT
King Eurystheus wanted Hippolyta's belt for his daughter, Admete.

destiny—a special purpose

In the tales of Wonder Woman, Queen Hippolyta was the proud mother of Diana, the champion of the Amazons. Hippolyta shaped her daughter's **destiny** in many ways. To bring Princess Diana into the world, Hippolyta first formed a baby out of clay. Then, with the help of the gods, she brought her daughter to life. From that day forward, Hippolyta helped train and mold Princess Diana into one of the world's greatest super heroes.

ANTIOPE

Antiope was also the daughter of the Greek god Ares. Her story, like that of her sister, Hippolyta, had a **tragic** ending. A prince named Theseus joined Hercules' task to steal Hippolyta's golden belt. As their army attacked Themiscyra, Antiope saw Theseus and fell in love. She then gave him the keys to the city, which allowed Hercules and his army to destroy Themiscyra.

Theseus and Antiope then moved to Athens — where Antiope's tragic end has been told in different ways. In one story, Theseus decided to marry another woman. Filled with jealousy, Antiope tried to kill his bride during the wedding. Instead, Theseus fought Antiope and killed her. In another tale, Antiope and Theseus married and had a son. But tragedy struck when the Amazons attacked Athens to take Antiope back. She was killed during the rescue attempt by another Amazon's arrow.

Long before Wonder Woman was born, the gods of Olympus made Hippolyta and Antiope the queens of the Amazons. Queen Antiope had a quicker temper than Hippolyta, but the two sisters ruled together peacefully for centuries. That changed when Hercules and his army attacked Themyscira and destroyed the city.

Half of the Amazons, led by Antiope, cried out for revenge and battled Hercules' army. The rest of the Amazons stayed with Queen Hippolyta and made a new home on a secret island, also named Themyscira. Antiope and her followers took the name Bana-Mighdall and became the "Lost Tribe of Amazons." They moved to a hidden city in Egypt.

FACT
In Greek myth, the Amazons' home is spelled "Themiscyra." In Wonder Woman lore, it is "Themyscira."

tragic—**extremely unfortunate, or disastrous**

CHAPTER 4
Mighty Men and Magicians

HERCULES

In Greek and Roman mythology, Hercules was a great hero and one of the strongest men on Earth. His father was the mighty god Zeus, and his mother was a mortal named Alcmene. Hercules was a helper to both the gods and humankind. Yet he led a difficult life and faced many **obstacles** from angry gods and mortals alike.

Upon Hercules' birth, the goddess Hera became enraged. She ordered a pair of snakes to kill him in his cradle. Fortunately, the infant used his great strength to kill the snakes with his bare hands. When Hercules was older, Hera arranged for him to serve King Eurystheus. The king ordered Hercules to perform 12 difficult tasks, known as labors. These included fighting the nine-headed Hydra, killing a man-eating lion, and cleaning the royal stables — which hadn't been cleaned in more than 30 years! Hercules used his strength to redirect the waters of a mighty river to wash out the stables.

In the world of Wonder Woman, Hercules was best known for attacking the city of Themyscira. Even though he had done it under the influence of Ares, the gods of Olympus decided that Hercules must be punished. Zeus sentenced Hercules to hold the weight of the Amazons' new island home on his shoulders for 3,000 years. Afterward, Hercules became the first man to set foot on their island. He begged for forgiveness, which the Amazons granted. Hercules then rose to Mount Olympus and became a god.

DEATH OF A HERO

In Greek myth, Hercules died as dramatically as he lived. It happened after he shot a **centaur** with a poisoned arrow. As the centaur lay dying, he gave his shirt to Hercules' wife. She encouraged Hercules to wear it, but the poison in the fabric slowly started to kill Hercules. In order to end his life more quickly, Hercules uprooted several trees, set them on fire, and climbed into the flames. Although his body perished, Hercules was granted immortal life on Mount Olympus.

obstacle—something that gets in the way or prevents someone from doing something

centaur—a creature with the head and chest of a human and the body of a horse

RAMA

Hindu mythology developed in India thousands of years ago, and those myths are incredibly complex. For instance, Vishnu was an all-powerful, blue-skinned god of protection who appeared on Earth in 10 different forms, known as avatars. His seventh avatar was the human named Rama. The power of Vishnu flowed through Rama and also turned his skin blue.

Rama was a prince and the **heir** to a kingdom, but his stepmother cheated him out of the throne. Rama's wife was then kidnapped by the 10-headed demon Ravana. Rama teamed up with the monkey god Hanuman, who gathered an army of monkeys and bears. Together, they battled Ravana's deadly army. In the end, Rama and Ravana faced off in single combat. Rama shot Ravana with a magic arrow and killed the demon.

In Wonder Woman's world, the power-hungry Greek god Cronus attempted to take control of the universe. Cronus formed an army to attack Mount Mandara, the sacred home of the Hindu gods. Rama traveled to Earth to seek Wonder Woman's help. When the two heroes confronted Cronus, the villain laughed and lifted a sharp blade that captured Rama and Wonder Woman's powers. It took the combined forces of the Olympian and Hindu gods and goddesses to defeat Cronus. Wonder Woman then destroyed the dangerous blade.

FACT
Hindu gods traveled on unusual creatures. Vishnu flew on Garuda, who was half-man and half-bird. The elephant-headed god Ganehsa traveled on a rat!

heir—someone who has been, or will be, left money, property, or a title

MERLIN

In ancient Britain, the Celts told amazing tales of King Arthur of Camelot and his Knights of the Round Table. Arthur's most trusted adviser was Merlin, a powerful wizard with a long, white beard. Merlin was the child of a mortal woman and a demon. He **inherited** the ability to shape-shift from his father. Merlin tutored young Arthur for many years. He also created Excalibur, an enchanted sword that was buried deep within a stone. It was widely believed that the first person to remove the sword would become the King of England. Hundreds of strong men tried and failed at the task. Finally, Arthur stepped up to the stone and easily removed the sword. The cheering crowd chose Arthur as their king.

In Wonder Woman's world, there was a time when Merlin fell under an evil spell that turned his beard black. He magically sent King Arthur and his loyal knight, Lancelot, through time and banished them to the 20th century. Wonder Woman came to their rescue and escorted them back to 6th century Camelot.

FACT
Some myths claimed that Merlin built the ancient British monument known as Stonehenge.

Merlin called down bolts of lightning to defeat Wonder Woman, but his plan backfired. One lighting bolt bounced off Wonder Woman's bracelets and knocked Merlin to the ground. With Wonder Woman's help, the evil spell was lifted.

CONCLUSION

Princess Diana became the champion of Themyscira because she was the strongest, the fastest, and the smartest of the Amazons. All hopes for defeating the war god Ares and saving mankind rested on her shoulders. Since then, she has bravely fought other evildoers in her mission to protect us all. She is a tireless champion, inspired by the mightiest Greek heroes of myth. The heroes of mythology may be centuries old, but they live on in the tales of Wonder Woman!

inherit—to receive a characteristic from parents

GLOSSARY

centaur (SEN-tor)—a creature with the head and chest of a human and the body of a horse

deity (DEE-uh-tee)—a god or goddess

destiny (DES-tih-nee)—a special purpose

eternal (i-TUR-nuhl)—lasting forever

forge (FORJ)—to form something from metal using heat or a hammer

heir (air)—someone who has been, or will be, left money, property, or a title

immortal (i-MOR-tuhl)—able to live forever

inherit (in-HER-it)—to receive a characteristic from parents

lore (LORE)—stories passed down over generations

mortal (MOR-tuhl)—human, referring to a being who will eventually die

mourn (MORN)—to be very sad and miss someone who has died

obstacle (OB-stuh-kuhl)—something that gets in the way or prevents someone from doing something

revenge (rih-VENJ)—an action taken to repay harm done

rival (RYE-vuhl)—someone whom a person competes against

solemn (SOL-uhm)—very serious

tragic (TRAJ-ik)—extremely unfortunate, or disastrous

READ MORE

Hoena, Blake. *The 12 Labors of Hercules: A Graphic Retelling.* Ancient Myths. North Mankato, Minn.: Capstone Press, 2015.

Hibbert, Clare. *Terrible Tales of Ancient Greece.* Monstrous Myths. New York: Gareth Stevens Publishing, 2014.

Krieg, Katherine. *What We Get from Greek Mythology.* Mythology and Culture. Ann Arbor, Mich.: Cherry Lake Publishing, 2015.

Nardo, Don. *Odysseus.* A Kid's Guide to Mythology. Hockessin, Del.: Mitchell Lane Publishers, 2016.

INTERNET SITES

FactHound offers a safe, fun way to find Internet sites related to this book. All of the sites on FactHound have been researched by our staff.

Here's all you do:

Visit *www.facthound.com*

Type in this code: 9781515745853

Check out projects, games and lots more at
www.capstonekids.com

INDEX